# Backyard Birds of Winter

## CAROL LERNER

*Morrow Junior Books • New York*

*For David Harrison,*
*founder of the Three Ash Nature Center*

*Watercolors were used for the full-color illustrations.*
*The text type is 13.5-point Caslon 540.*

*Printed in the United States of America.*

*1  2  3  4  5  6  7  8  9  10*

*Library of Congress Cataloging-in-Publication Data*
*Lerner, Carol.    Backyard birds of winter/Carol Lerner.*
*p.    cm.*
*Includes bibliographical references and index.*
*ISBN 0-688-12819-X (trade)—ISBN 0-688-12820-3 (library)*
*1. Birds—North America.*
*2. Birds—Wintering—North America.    I. Title.*
*QL681.L44   1994   598.2973—dc20*
*94-3036   CIP*

# CONTENTS

Introduction: Birds in Winter   4

Chickadees and Titmice   9

Cardinal   11

Climbers   12

Blackbirds   16

Carolina Wren   19

Mimics   20

Two Thrushes   22

Mourning Dove   24

Immigrants   25

Sparrows and Juncos   28

Rufous-sided Towhee   31

Jays, Crows, and Magpies   32

Everyday Finches   36

Wanderers   38

Bird Food and Bird Feeders   41

Project FeederWatch   45

For Further Reading   46

Index   47

# INTRODUCTION: BIRDS IN WINTER

Most wild animals are fearful of human beings and try to stay at a safe distance. To observe them, we must be secret watchers, silent and unseen. But wild birds are different. Many of them are willing to live close to people, and some will come right to our doorsteps. If we offer food, they come regularly and often.

Growing numbers of people have discovered the pleasures of feeding birds in winter. There is a feeling of satisfaction in helping them to survive this difficult season. The lifeless yard fills with color and action as birds line up at the feeder. Without the leaves of summer to hide them, they stand in full view. And, because many birds live in flocks during the wintertime, they come in groups rather than one by one.

Although many birds fly off to the tropics or the deep South at the end of summer, no part of the country is without winter birds. Some of the feeder customers are permanent residents of the area, year-round birds that stay to nest and raise their young the following spring and summer. Others are winter visitors, migrating birds that nest farther north but shift southward for the winter. Still another group falls somewhere in the middle: Some members of these species fly south, while smaller numbers stay behind.

The least predictable of all the winter visitors are the wanderers, northern seed-eating birds that make surprise winter appearances that are known as irruptions. These species have no regular pattern of migration. They may appear in occasional years—or not at all.

It is a challenge for small birds to last through the winter, especially in the cold climates of the North. Squirrels and raccoons settle down in warm nests on subzero or stormy days, waiting for better weather before they go out for food. But birds must be out and feeding every day to stay alive and to keep their bodies warm. And the smaller the bird, the greater the danger that it may freeze to death. The bodies of small birds have more surface area, ounce for ounce of weight, than larger birds do. And every square inch of body surface continually loses heat into the cold air, night and day.

Birds can endure cold because they are covered by an outstanding insulating material. Under a smooth outer layer of feathers lies a mass of soft down that traps and holds warm air next to the skin. Birds are able to fluff their down when necessary, making the layer of insulation even thicker and more protective. Some northern birds also have winter coats with more feathers than they have in summer.

A few body parts—bills, legs, and feet—are bare. However, unlike human noses and toes, these are not fleshy and do not freeze easily. In many birds, the thin arteries bringing warm blood down through the legs are right next to the veins that return cold blood to the main part of the body. Heat passes from the warm blood to the cold and keeps the blood in the veins above the freezing point.

You may sometimes see a bird trying to warm a cold beak or leg. The bird will tuck its head beneath its wing or stand on one foot while pulling the other leg close to its breast feathers. Small birds feeding in the cold often squat low to the ground, bringing their legs closer to their warm bodies.

Some birds have a more unusual way of surviving in extreme cold. The chickadee, for one, can conserve body heat by slowing down its body processes at night. Its temperature drops 13° Fahrenheit, and its breathing slows from 95 to 65 breaths a minute.

The more common way for a bird to save body heat overnight is to rest in a protected place out of the chill wind. Woodpeckers and chickadees stay in tree holes. Many birds find shelter in evergreen trees and bushes or in old bird nests, and some roost in the company of other birds to share body warmth.

But saving body heat is only part of survival. The bird first needs to produce heat, and that requires food. Birds do not die from cold if they get enough to eat. But even where the winter is mild, food is harder to find than it is during the growing season. Insects are out of sight, and the only plant food is the seeds and fruits still remaining from last summer.

The normal temperatures of birds range from 101° to 112° Fahrenheit, higher than the body temperatures of mammals. During daylight hours a bird must eat enough to keep its body warm until the next morning and to fuel all the activities of the day. Short winter days are barely long enough to find that much food. Small birds must eat almost constantly from dawn to nightfall.

Birds digest their food quickly. A sparrow's food passes through its digestive system in an hour and a half. Because their body processes are so rapid, birds are able to store up a layer of fat each day and burn it for fuel that night.

Some northern seed eaters are also able to set aside an extra supply of food for the night. One of these is the redpoll, a bird of the far North. Redpolls have storage places inside their throats. After eating all they can, they pack more seeds into the throat pouches and eat these later in the night.

Some birds seem to spend so much time at feeding stations that people fear they will starve without human help. But birds do not normally depend upon feeders for most of their winter needs. Studies of the black-capped chickadee, a common and regular backyard visitor in the East, show that it takes only about one-fourth of its food from feeders. For the rest, the chickadee finds dormant insects, insect eggs, and tree seeds.

Feeders take on greater importance in periods of extreme cold, or when a blanket of snow or ice covers the normal food sources. In periods of severe weather, well-stocked feeders might make the difference between death and survival. They will certainly make the birds' lives a little easier.

Many of the birds seen at feeders have changed their winter patterns. Some southern species have moved farther north, and birds that used to migrate now stay behind and face the winter cold. The growing number of feeding stations must be one reason for these changing patterns. Another may be the milder winters of the past century.

Large-scale changes in the use of land certainly affect birds' habits as well. Forests and farms become housing developments and factories, wetlands are drained, and other farms are abandoned and begin to fill with trees again. Birds must adjust to the changed habitat or search for new places to live.

Even if you put out a variety of bird foods, you may still be disappointed by the visitors that come. Unless your neighborhood offers some good bird habitats, you cannot expect to attract many different kinds of birds. You are likely to see a wider variety if you live near a large park, a woodland, cultivated fields, or a river or lake (if not frozen over). Suburbs with generous plantings of trees and shrubs are now home to many birds that once lived on the edges of forests. In the inner city, you may have to be satisfied with only three or four common kinds of birds—but you will still enjoy watching them.

This book describes the most common visitors to winter feeders in the lower forty-eight states and southern Canada. About a third of the species are very widespread. The others are common only in some regions. In the case of the latter, a small map next to each bird's picture shows where it lives in winter.

Except where the bird's length appears next to its picture, birds are shown about three-fourths their actual size.

Look in the back of the book for some suggestions about bird feeders and the kinds of food with which to fill them.

TUFTED TITMOUSE

BLACK-CAPPED CHICKADEE

# CHICKADEES AND TITMICE

The yard bursts into life when the chickadees come. Three to six or more may appear at once. Tufted titmice and other small birds often travel with them and may arrive at the same time.

Chickadees and titmice are members of the same family and close relatives. The difference between them is that titmice have pointed crests on their heads.

They even have the same habits: They are busy and curious and are always moving. Like acrobats, they swing from twig to twig and may hang head down while exploring the tip of a branch. They stay in little groups all winter long, and most do not migrate.

In the backyard they are snatch-and-grab feeders. They swoop to the feeder to carry off a sunflower seed. Holding the seed with their toes, they smash the shell, eat the kernel, and rush back for another.

The black-capped chickadee is the most widespread chickadee in the United States.

Fifty years ago the tufted titmouse lived only in the southeastern states. It has moved northward and now is familiar in the Northeast and in the Great Lakes region.

In the southeastern states the Carolina chickadee takes the place of the black-capped. The Carolina is a little smaller but very similar in appearance. Where the ranges of the two birds meet, the best way to tell them apart is to listen to the male sing. The Carolina's song is faster, and the notes have a higher pitch.

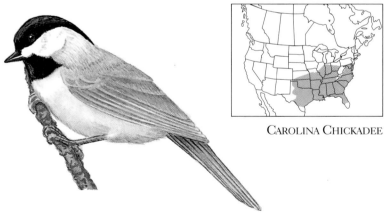

CAROLINA CHICKADEE

Compared to the look-alike black-capped chickadee, the Carolina chickadee has less white on the outer edges of its wings and paler color on its sides.

Feeders in the West are visited by chestnut-backed and mountain chickadees, as well as the black caps. Chestnut-backed chickadees live in mountain areas along the Pacific coast.

CHESTNUT-BACKED CHICKADEE

The mountain chickadee is the only chickadee with a white stripe above the eye. These birds nest at high elevations but come down to the foothills for winter. They sometimes join up with groups of black caps to form a mixed flock.

MOUNTAIN CHICKADEE

PLAIN TITMOUSE

The plain titmouse is a bird of the warm Southwest. Unlike the eastern tufted titmouse, it usually travels alone or in pairs.

NORTHERN CARDINAL

# CARDINAL

In spite of its name, the northern cardinal was originally a bird of the southern states. Over the past century, however, cardinals have moved steadily northward. They now live in almost every part of the eastern United States.

Cardinals mate for life. The pair stays together all year in the same place, and some of their offspring may remain with them over the winter. They often visit winter feeders in flocks of mixed males and females.

Cardinals are fond of sunflower seeds. Using their tongues, they roll the seed into position, crack it in their powerful beaks, and drop the shell as they eat the kernel.

Male cardinals are usually the brightest birds at winter feeders. The females' feathers are a duller brown with red tints. Both have black face masks and orange-red beaks. Cardinals are one of the few birds that may break into song even in the dead of winter.

# CLIMBERS

A woodpecker's body is made for climbing trees and digging into wood. Other kinds of birds have four toes on each foot—three in front and one in back. But most woodpeckers have two toes pointing forward and two pointing back. The two pairs of toes work like a clamp, making it easier for the bird to cling to the side of a tree. The tail helps too. Stiff, pointed tail feathers support the bird's weight as it hammers the tree with its bill.

A woodpecker's bill is big and heavy, and the bones in its head are thicker and stronger than those of other birds. The heavy skull is like a football helmet, protecting the bird's eyes and brain as it pounds on trees. The woodpecker's long tongue can reach deep into holes, picking up insects hidden in the wood.

All woodpeckers are attracted to suet at feeders.

Downy woodpeckers are the most common woodpeckers at feeders. A pair of downies that nests in the summer usually stays together through the year, so you may see both the male and female in your yard. You will be able to recognize the male by the patch of red on the back of his head.

Hairy woodpeckers look like downies, except that they are a little larger. The easiest way to tell the two species apart is by the size of the bill.

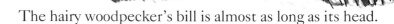

The hairy woodpecker's bill is almost as long as its head.

RED-BELLIED
WOODPECKER

Red-bellied woodpeckers actually have very little red on their bellies. They have zebra-striped backs and bright orange-red heads. They used to live only in the southeastern states, but they have been moving farther and farther north in the last hundred years. Now they are found all over the East.

Red-bellied woodpeckers will often come to feeders for seeds as well as suet.

Unlike other woodpeckers, northern
flickers spend much of their time on the
ground, feeding on insects. They like
ants especially. Flickers have black bibs
under their chins and white rumps. You
see the white rump patch when they fly.

Eastern and western flickers have
different coloring on various parts of the
body. Only eastern birds—females as
well as males—have red patches on the
back of the head. All males have a mus-
tache, but it is black in eastern flickers
and red in western ones.

The shaft—the rib that runs down
the middle of a feather—has different
colors too. It is bright yellow on eastern
birds and red on most westerners.

14

Nuthatches, like woodpeckers, are expert climbers and spend most of their time on trees. They are upside-down birds, the only climbers that typically move headfirst down the trunks of trees. They have big heads and small tails on short streamlined bodies. The bill is almost as long as the head, but it is not strong enough to peck into wood or crack very hard nuts. Sunflower seeds are their favorite backyard food.

Nuthatches often attach themselves to winter flocks of chickadees and titmice. And, like them, the nuthatch is a snatch-and-grab feeder. It carries off a single seed to a nearby tree and shoves it into a crack of bark so it is held firmly in place. Then the bird hammers off the shell to reach the seed.

The white-breasted nuthatch is a year-round bird in all parts of its range.

The red-breasted nuthatch—smaller, and with a white eye line—usually lives in the evergreen forests of the far North and the West. In years when the cone-bearing trees produce few seeds, many red-breasted nuthatches move south for the winter and show up at feeders across the United States.

# Blackbirds

After the nesting season ends, blackbirds begin to gather in flocks before moving south for the winter. The flocks usually contain a mixture of different kinds of blackbirds, including red-winged blackbirds, grackles, and cowbirds.

Once they reach their wintering area, the birds break up into smaller groups each morning to search for food. In the afternoon they assemble again in a noisy crowd and move to a grove of trees to spend the night. A single roosting flock in the South may contain millions of birds.

While most red-winged blackbirds migrate, some stay in the northern states all winter. The number remaining is larger now, perhaps because growing numbers of bird feeders make it easier to get through winter.

Only the male redwing is black. Females are brown and streaked on the breast.

COMMON GRACKLE

The common grackle has a longer tail than the redwing. It has yellow eyes and black feathers that shine with glints of blue, purple, green, or bronze. Grackles are eastern blackbirds that migrate for the winter, but they too are changing their habits. Now they are moving farther north and west in summer, and like the redwings, some small flocks remain in the northern states during the cold months.

17

When buffalo roamed the prairie, brown-headed cowbirds followed in their footsteps. The herd stirred up insects as it moved through the grass, and the birds ate the insects. After cattle took the place of buffalo, the birds began to follow the cattle and became "cow" birds. Cowbirds also eat grains, seeds, and some fruits, such as berries.

Cowbirds are the only North American birds that use the nests of other birds for their young. A female cowbird spies on birds of other species when they are making their nests. When the cowbird finds a nest, she lays her own eggs there and leaves them for the other bird to raise.

Males have black bodies contrasting with brown heads. Females are a plain gray-brown.

BROWN-HEADED COWBIRD

CAROLINA WREN

## CAROLINA WREN

Although these are southern birds, some Carolina wrens from each new generation move farther north. They survive in mild winters, but many of the northern birds die in years of severe cold and heavy snow. When mild winters return to these areas, the wren population slowly builds up again.

Like all wrens, the Carolina has an upturned tail. It is the largest eastern wren. Its body is bright brown above and buff yellow below, and a broad white streak runs above each eye.

Even in winter, the wrens eat mostly insect food. At feeders they like suet and peanut butter mixtures.

# MIMICS

Most songbirds have several different calls. Birds belonging to the family of mimics (*Mimidae*) have an almost endless variety of songs, stringing together a long series of musical phrases.

No one is sure about the reasons for this behavior. Perhaps it frightens other birds away from the singer's territory. Or perhaps the females in this family are more likely to mate with a male having a long song.

Mimics are dull in color, with thin bills and long tails.

Northern mockingbirds imitate the songs of other kinds of birds. In a single outburst, their call may include the songs of a dozen or more different birds, as well as the bark of a dog, the croak of a frog, and the sound of a squeaky gate.

This is a southern bird that has slowly spread farther north and southwest. Many mockingbirds that summer in the northern parts of their range move south for winter, but some remain as far north as New England. They may try to chase other birds away from the feeder, regarding the whole yard as their private territory.

Mockingbirds usually ignore the seeds in a feeder, but they like apples, raisins, suet, and peanut butter mixtures.

NORTHERN MOCKINGBIRD

BROWN THRASHER

 

The brown thrasher is more secretive than its bold relative, the mockingbird. It feeds on the ground, often hidden beneath the bushes. The thrasher sorts through ground litter with its long bill, looking for insects, spiders, seeds, and small fruits.

Some thrashers live year-round in the Southeast, visiting winter feeders to eat grains and seeds, suet, and bits of dried fruit. Others nest in the North and move south for winter.

# TWO THRUSHES

All thrushes have spots on their breasts at some time in their lives. These two species have speckled breasts when young but lose the spots when they become adults.

The red-breasted American robin is the most familiar thrush in North America. Even though it is a migrating bird, growing numbers remain in the northern states through the winter. They may show up at winter feeders almost anywhere in the United States.

Still, most robins that spend the summer in Canada, the northern plains states, or the Great Lakes region do fly south. When they arrive at their winter homes, they often band together with local robins. Some winter flocks in the South contain thousands of birds.

In summer robins are a common sight as they hop across lawns, looking for worms. In fall they turn to fruits and berries for most of their food. They come to the feeder for raisins and apples, and they also like soft foods such as bread and suet.

AMERICAN ROBIN

VARIED THRUSH

The varied thrush looks much like a robin. It is sometimes called the banded robin because of the heavy black streak running across the male's breast. The male has an orange stripe through its eye and orange bars on its wings. Females are similar but paler in color.

The varied thrush lives in the wet forests of the Pacific coast. In winter it comes down from the mountains or migrates to the South.

Like the robin, it eats apples, bread, and suet at feeders.

# MOURNING DOVE

Mourning doves have also changed their habits in this century, moving farther and farther north for the spring nesting season. They fly south in fall, but now more doves stay in the northern states all through the year. Only the coldest parts of the country are without them in winter.

The bird is named for its call, but you won't hear it until spring comes. The male's song is a low, sad-sounding *coo*.

The mourning dove is a member of the pigeon family, but it is more slender and slightly smaller than the common pigeon. It has a long pointed tail, and its wings make a whistling sound in flight. Like other pigeons, the dove has short legs and a small head that bobs back and forth as it walks.

All doves and pigeons have a crop, or craw—a storage place in the throat. Mourning doves feed on the ground, picking up all kinds of small seeds from the surface and storing them in their crops. Unlike other ground-feeding birds, they can't scratch the earth to find buried food, because their feet are very tender. When the crop is filled, they fly off to sit quietly while the seeds they've gathered slowly move from the crop to the stomach to be digested.

# IMMIGRANTS

A few backyard birds have come from distant lands. In the 1700s and 1800s many organizations and private people set out to add foreign animals to the stock of North American wildlife. Hunters imported game birds. Some people who had come to America from Europe missed seeing the birds of their homelands and brought in foreign songbirds. Finally, in 1900, the United States passed the Lacey Act, making it illegal to import animals and release them into the wild. Most birds turned loose in a new country soon disappear, unable to find food and shelter in strange surroundings. But pigeons, house sparrows, and starlings are champion survivors.

They prefer to live near people, but they are not very popular birds. They gather in flocks that carry disease, leave heaps of droppings on buildings, and destroy some fruit and grain crops. Efforts to reduce their numbers have not had much success. It seems they are here to stay.

The ancestor of the pigeon is the wild rock dove, a bird that nests on cliffs in Europe, Africa, and Asia. The rock dove was tamed probably before the end of the Stone Age. For thousands of years people raised domesticated pigeons for food.

Pigeons first came to the United States with early European settlers, most likely around 1621. Today's pigeons are feral—that is, domesticated animals that have gone back to the wild. But even these pigeons usually stay near human homes. As the frontier moved westward across North America, the number of feral pigeons grew, and they moved with the settlers.

Length: 11 inches

25

The house sparrow, or English sparrow, is native to Europe and parts of Asia and northern Africa. It is not a close relative of the native North American sparrows.

House sparrows were brought to the United States by the Brooklyn Institute in 1851, in the hope that they would control an outbreak of caterpillars. The first birds did not live, but fifty more were released two years later. These survived and began to raise young. In the next thirty or forty years, imported house sparrows were set free in a hundred different cities in thirty-nine states.

They spread out quickly to other towns and cities, often following the paths laid by roads and railroad tracks. They even hitchhiked on paddleboats sailing down large American rivers. By 1900 they were the most common bird in North America.

House sparrows were thought of as pests in England for more than a century before the first ones were brought to the United States—and for good reason. The flocks destroy fruit and grain, and they spread disease to farmyard birds. By the late 1800s, they were declared pests in several states and rewards were paid for killing them. They were even put on the menu in some restaurants.

Their numbers went down after 1920. As cars took the place of horses and wagons, city birds no longer had spilled oats and horse droppings to eat. However, they still thrive where grain is grown and livestock is raised. Today their numbers are highest in Illinois, Indiana, and Ohio.

House sparrows have thicker beaks than the native sparrows. The male has a black bib that is pale in winter but becomes dark by spring. The female's back is streaked with brown. She has a plain breast and a pale line through the eyes.

The European starling was the last of these three species to get a foothold in North America. In the late 1800s starlings were set free in at least five different American states and in Quebec, but only a few survived.

In the 1880s a man who loved Shakespeare decided that he would bring every bird species mentioned by the poet to the United States. He released starlings in New York City in 1890 and 1891. By 1950 they had spread over the entire United States and throughout southern Canada and were one of the most numerous birds in North America.

When starlings arrive at feeders, they often chase other birds away. They nest in tree holes and other cavities and sometimes push out native woodpeckers, swallows, and bluebirds from these nesting places.

Starlings get their name from their winter appearance. In late summer they grow a fresh set of feathers with white tips, making them look spotted or speckled with little "stars." By spring most of the white tips have worn off, and the bird is plain shiny black.

# SPARROWS AND JUNCOS

Sparrows are small seed-eating birds with brown-streaked backs. In the wild and in the yard, they prefer to feed on the ground. In winter sparrows travel in flocks that may number five or ten birds or, in the case of tree sparrows and chipping sparrows, forty or fifty. There are many kinds of sparrows, and some of them are very hard to tell apart, but only a few species are likely to be seen at winter feeders.

American tree sparrows fly down from the Arctic to spend winter in the northern United States. They are usually found in fields and shrubs rather than in trees. The American bird got its name because both it and the European tree sparrow have reddish caps, and people thought they were the same species. An American tree sparrow can be recognized by the black spot in the center of its plain gray breast.

The song sparrow also has a central spot, but its white breast has brown streaks. Song sparrows vary in size and color, depending upon where they live. Instead of brown, its color may be grayish or a deep red-brown, and some birds are paler and have less streaking on the breast.

Fox sparrows are named for their color, a bright rusty brown resembling the coat of a red fox. But, like song sparrows, fox sparrows vary in color, and western birds are darker brown. All have heavy streaks on the breast, and most have reddish tails and a large spot in the middle of the breast. They are larger than most song sparrows.

SONG SPARROW

FOX SPARROW

TREE SPARROW

CHIPPING SPARROW

The chipping sparrow has no breast marks. It has a brick-red cap, a broad white streak below the cap, and a narrow black line through each eye. Chipping sparrows are widespread in summer but move to the lower South for winter.

The Harris's sparrow nests in the bogs of northern Canada and winters in the central part of the United States. The largest of all the sparrows, it is easily identified by its black crown, face, and throat.

HARRIS'S SPARROW

WHITE-CROWNED SPARROW

WHITE-THROATED SPARROW

Most white-crowned sparrows and white-throated sparrows also nest far north and migrate south. Both birds have white throat patches, but you can tell them apart by the color of their bills—pink or yellow for whitecrowns, dark for whitethroats. Adult whitethroats also have a small patch of yellow in front of each eye.

Dark-eyed juncos are also called snowbirds, because their arrival from northern nesting places indicates that winter is on the way. Juncos are the feeder champions: They are seen at more backyard feeding stations than are any other bird species.

They come in different colors. Eastern birds are usually gray on the head, breast, and back, while western juncos have black or gray heads and breasts with brown backs. But it is easy to spot a junco of any color. Just look for its pink bill and watch its tail; a junco flicks its tail constantly, on the ground or in flight. As it does, you will see a long white feather on each side of the tail.

# RUFOUS-SIDED TOWHEE

Towhees come to backyards, but they are rather secretive. They often stay on the edges, under the cover of bushes, looking for seeds on the ground. Like some of their sparrow relatives, they take little forward hops and then jump back, scraping the ground with both feet to uncover fallen seeds. You often hear scratching long before you see them.

At feeders they eat seeds, cracked corn, and suet.

A dozen or more towhees may join in a winter flock. Sometimes they mix with cardinals, sparrows, and other birds.

The rufous-sided towhee in the West looks a little different from the eastern ones illustrated here. Western birds have bands of white in their wings and white spots on their backs. Some birds in the southeastern United States have white eyes instead of red.

Females have brown heads, backs, and tails.

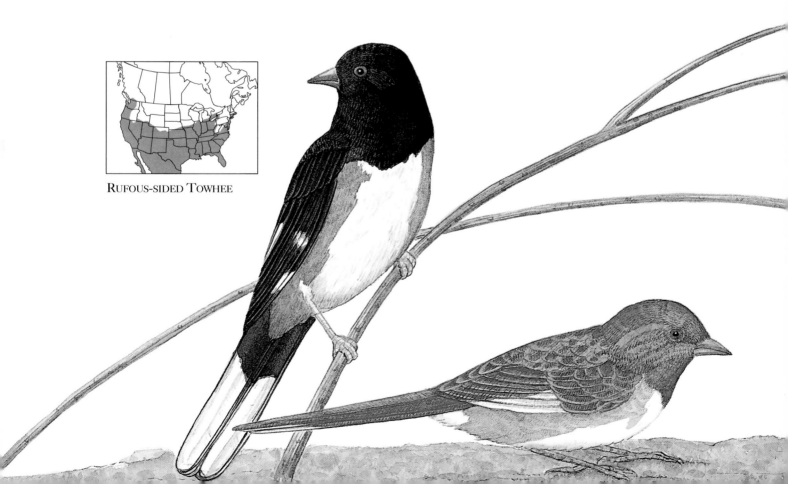

RUFOUS-SIDED TOWHEE

# JAYS, CROWS, AND MAGPIES

All of these birds belong to the crow family. They are noisy, bold, and smart, often giving early warning to other wildlife by screaming at the first sign of danger. They are also thieves and killers. If one of them sees another bird hiding seeds or acorns, it will rush to the spot when the first bird leaves and try to steal the food. And in nesting season they sometimes eat the eggs and young of other birds.

Blue jays are year-round birds east of the Rocky Mountains, and they are slowly spreading farther west. In winter they usually travel in pairs or in small groups. At feeders the blue jay sometimes stuffs its throat with food and flies off to hide it under roof shingles, leaves, or in old bird nests.

BLUE JAY

A scrub jay is about the size of a blue jay but without the pointed crest on the head. Most scrub jays live in the West. Farmers and fruit growers blame them for serious crop damage, and until the 1930s they were killed in organized shoots.

A second, much smaller population of scrub jays lives in central Florida, completely separated from the western birds. Florida scrub jays have been disappearing as more and more of their sandy scrub habitat is turned into orchards, housing, and malls.

Stellar's jay is a bird of the western North American forest, the only western jay with a crest. Some of these forest birds move to more open country in winter and become regular feeder visitors. Like other jays, the Stellar's stores food, especially acorns and sunflower seeds.

Length: 11 inches

STELLAR'S JAY

Crows sometimes eat ripe crops, and like other members of the crow family, they rob birds' nests. Because of this, they have been attacked by farmers, hunters, and even bird lovers, who have used guns, poison, traps, and dynamite to kill them. Large flocks of crows gather on winter nights to roost in trees, making them easy targets.

The American crow is the most widespread member of its family in the United States and is present in most parts of the country in winter. It is familiar in suburbs and city parks as well as in woodlands and on farms. Crows visit backyards in small or large groups to feed on the ground.

Length: 17 inches

Length: 18 inches

BLACK-BILLED MAGPIE

You can't confuse the magpie with any other bird. The black-billed magpie is a large black-and-white bird with a long tail that makes up half of its length. The dark wings and tail have a greenish tint in the sunlight.

The magpie comes to feeders in open areas but does not like to feed under trees. Like other family members, magpies will eat almost anything they find, including garbage.

This western bird lives as far north as Alaska. They are year-round birds in their home areas, but in winter some magpies wander eastward as far as the midwestern states.

# Everyday Finches

House finches and goldfinches are common feeder visitors throughout most of the United States. If you keep your feeder filled with seeds, you can expect to see them every day. In the wintertime they almost always arrive as part of a flock.

Like other finches, they have heavy cone-shaped beaks for eating seeds. A special groove inside the beak holds the seed in place as strong jaws crack the husk. These birds do not leave the feeder in a hurry. They usually settle in and eat and eat until they have had their fill of niger (NI-jer) and sunflower seeds. Even when there is plenty of room at the feeder, they squabble with one another for the best perch.

The American goldfinch, like all birds, sheds its feathers in fall and grows a new set for winter. The male loses his black cap and bright yellow body feathers. Both sexes are a dull yellow during the winter.

But unlike most birds, the goldfinch has a second molt each year. As spring approaches, a new set of feathers grows in. In late winter you can see the gradual change on some males at your feeder. Patches of gold body feathers and jet-black caps begin to appear again.

The house finch was originally a western bird. In the early 1940s some caged finches from California were set free on New York's Long Island. They spread rapidly, for, like house sparrows, house finches thrive in towns and cities. Now they are common on both sides of the continent. The eastern house finches range from the Atlantic coast to the Mississippi River and beyond, and they are still spreading westward. They are year-round birds.

HOUSE FINCH

# WANDERERS

Some seed-eating finches of the northern forests depend upon the cones of pines, spruces, and other evergreen trees for winter food. In years when there is a small crop of cones, hunger drives them from home. They have no regular migration route that they follow each year. It is always a surprise when purple finches, pine siskins, or redpolls show up at a feeding station.

Like house finches and goldfinches, these small northern finches travel in flocks, and the group may contain a mix of different species. When they find a feeder heaped with food, they are likely to stay and empty it before moving on.

The purple finch looks much like its close relative, the house finch. Female purple finches have a strong brown-and-white face pattern, however, and female house finches do not. Male purple finches lack the heavy brown streaks that mark the sides of male house finches.

PURPLE FINCH

Pine siskins are closely related to goldfinches. Siskins are streaked with brown. There are touches of yellow in the wings and tail, but the yellow is not always easy to see. Sometimes a siskin will try to scare other birds away from the feeder by opening its mouth wide and raising its wing feathers. Then you can see the yellow patches.

Common redpolls visiting feeders in lower Canada and the northern United States have traveled a great distance in search of food, for they nest in the far Arctic regions.

Redpolls have red caps and black chins. Males have pink breasts. They are closely related to pine siskins and goldfinches and sometimes flock with the siskins.

COMMON REDPOLL

Evening grosbeaks live in the forests of the North and West, eating the seeds and fruits of woodland trees in winter. In years of food shortage they may stray as far south as Texas and Georgia, suddenly appearing in yards where they have never before been seen.

Grosbeaks have oversized beaks that are strong enough to crack a cherry pit. They have a great taste for sunflower seeds and may sit at the feeder for an hour, husking and eating until the tray is picked clean.

Females look like males that have been dipped in silver-gray paint. They are much duller in color and lack the bright yellow face mark.

# BIRD FOOD AND BIRD FEEDERS

## *Food*

Now that bird feeding is so popular, seed can be bought at almost any supermarket. You may find that a sack of supermarket feed fits your needs and your birds' needs perfectly. Or you may find that the birds coming to your yard pick out the bits they like and leave the rest behind.

Ready-made mixes usually contain a lot of wheat, buckwheat, milo (sorghum), and other "filler" seeds and grains that few birds like. If you find you are throwing away food because the birds won't touch it, you may want to mix your own. Sacks containing just one kind of seed or grain can be bought at many hardware stores and garden shops.

Sunflower seeds are easy to find. There are two kinds, striped seeds and the smaller black oil seeds. Both will vanish from your feeder quickly, but some small birds have trouble cracking the larger seeds. Black oil seeds have thinner shells and contain more oil, providing the birds with more fat and therefore more energy.

A wide variety of birds eat cracked corn. Feed corn labeled "finely cracked" is probably best, because even small birds can eat it. Cracked corn is sold at some feed and hardware stores and at bird specialty stores.

Millet is a grass seed. The seeds are small and round, either white or red. Small seed-eaters like both kinds, although it is said they prefer the white.

If you make your own mix, check your feeder for leftovers and adjust the proportions to the birds' preferences. For ground-feeding birds, try a mixture of four parts cracked corn to one part millet and one part sunflower seeds. If you do use a ready-made mix, look for one that has the largest amount of these three items and the least filler.

Goldfinches love niger seed, which is often called thistle seed in the stores. The tiny black seed, rich in oil, comes from Africa and is expensive. Niger seed must be served in special feeders (see page 43).

The best way to attract woodpeckers is to put out a supply of pure fat, which is a good substitute for insect food. The best and easiest fat to use is beef suet; it is flaky and crumbles nicely as the birds peck at it. However, it is not always easy to find at the butcher shop. Other kinds of beef fat are said to be tougher and stringier, but woodpeckers—as well as titmice and chickadees—will not turn it down. You can also buy suet cakes (melted fat mixed with seeds) where bird-feeding supplies are sold, but they cost more.

Once the weather turns warm, suet and other beef fats begin to drip and turn rancid and should be thrown away.

Birds also like many of the same foods we do. They enjoy peanut butter, but a small bird can choke if the peanut butter sticks in its throat. Peanut butter for birds should be mixed with cornmeal and some kind of solid fat, such as the drippings from bacon or a meat roast. Mix one part peanut butter and one part fat with six parts cornmeal.

Some people put out a variety of other treats: chopped nuts, bits of hard cheese, crumbled doughnuts, raisins, and so on.

## Water

Birds need water at all times of the year. Seed-eaters have the greatest need because their food contains very little moisture. You often see birds taking a drink by eating snow.

Providing water in winter is difficult because, of course, the water turns to ice. Some people run out and add hot water to the birdbath every time it freezes over. If you want to offer water in freezing weather, the best way is to use a heater made especially for birdbaths. They are sold in some stores that carry bird supplies and in some specialty mail-order catalogs.

Pole-mounted feeder with plastic baffle

## Feeders

Dozens of different kinds of feeders are sold. You can spend a little or a lot for one, or you can make your own.

The simplest way to feed birds is to scatter food on the ground. Some of the seed will be lost in the dirt, soaked by rain, or covered by snow; and the seed may attract hungry mice or rats to your yard. If you have squirrels in your neighborhood, they may end up with most of the food.

Birds that feed on the ground will accept a low feeding place (a board or the flat side of a split log) a few inches off the ground. This makes clean-up easier but does not solve the rat and squirrel problem.

Birds that like to eat on the ground also come to pole-mounted feeders. One advantage of using a pole or wooden post is that it puts the feeder up at window level so you can see the birds better. Squirrels are great climbers, but if you slip a curved piece of sheet metal or a section of plastic pipe around the pole, you may keep them (and raccoons) from climbing the post. Another solution is to mount a baffle—a smooth disk or cone that offers no foothold—on the pole just below the feeder. You can buy a baffle at bird-supply shops or make your own out of a metal garbage-can cover.

A roof on the pole-top feeder will protect the food from snow and rain.

If you have a convenient tree nearby, you can hang a feeder. Transparent plastic feeders come in a variety of shapes, usually cylinders or globes, with perches so several birds can eat at once. Many kinds of wooden feeders are also sold. You can make your own from a cardboard milk carton, a plastic soda bottle, or scraps of wood.

Hanging feeders are good for holding an assortment of seeds—mixed or sunflower or niger. Feeders for niger seed have very small holes, just large enough for a small finch to pick out a single seed.

Squirrels reach hanging feeders too and sometimes chew holes in plastic ones to reach the food. Try to place the feeder far enough from other tree branches so the squirrels cannot jump over to it. Using plastic rope or wire to hang the feeder may pre-

Milk carton seed feeder

vent them from climbing down to the food. If not, you will have to string a lightweight baffle above the feeder on the line that holds it. Some hanging

Hanging suet feeder basket

feeders come with plastic roofs that act as baffles.

To hang up pieces of fat, you can use plastic net bags in which onions and oranges are sold. Or you can use plastic-coated wire baskets that are sold specifically for this purpose. They are available at stores that sell bird feeders. The holders can be either hung or attached to posts or tree trunks.

Tree trunks are also good for serving peanut butter mixtures. Just smear the mix on the bark.

Whatever feed you use, you should keep the feeder clean. Moldy food and bird droppings can carry disease. Throw away any spoiled food and scrub your feeders when they are dirty.

## Cover

Trees and bushes around the feeders give birds a place to perch and take cover from danger. They also act as windbreaks. At the same time, they provide jumping-off points for squirrels trying to reach the food and hiding places for cats waiting to pounce on the birds.

You have to balance these considerations when you pick a spot for your feeder. You may be able to make the area safer simply by trimming off some nearby branches.

If there is no cover at all near your feeder, you might collect some old Christmas trees after the holiday and place them around your yard.

# PROJECT FEEDERWATCH

Keeping track of backyard birds can be more than an interesting hobby. It can also help us to discover what is happening to our birds.

Thousands of people who feed birds in the United States and Canada take part in Project FeederWatch by keeping records of visitors to their winter feeders. These records show changing winter ranges and make us aware of rising or falling bird populations.

FeederWatchers pay a small fee each year and receive newsletters and special forms for their reports. To learn more, write to Project FeederWatch, Cornell Laboratory of Ornithology, 159 Sapsucker Woods Road, Ithaca, NY 14850.

# FOR FURTHER READING

## Identifying the Birds

National Geographic Society. *Birds of North America*. Washington, DC: National Geographic Society, 1983.

Peterson, Roger Tory. *A Field Guide to Eastern Birds*. Boston: Houghton Mifflin, 1984.

_____. *A Field Guide to Western Birds*. Boston: Houghton Mifflin, 1984.

Robbins, Chandler, Bertel Bruun, Herbert Zim, and Arthur Singer. *Birds of North America*. New York: Golden Press/Western Publishing, 1986.

## Feeding the Birds

Burton, Robert. *North American Birdfeeder Handbook*. New York: Dorling Kindersley, 1992.

Dennis, John V. *A Complete Guide to Bird Feeding*. New York: Alfred A. Knopf, 1988.

_____. *A Guide to Western Bird Feeding*. Marietta, OH: Bird Watcher's Digest Press, 1991.

Kress, Stephen W. *The Audubon Society Guide to Attracting Birds*. New York: Scribner's, 1985.

Waldon, Bob. *A Guide to Feeding Winter Birds*. Stillwater, MN: Voyageur Press, 1991.

There are many more books about bird feeding. Check the shelves of your local library.

# INDEX

Illustrations are in **boldface**.

acorns, 32, 33

baffle, **42,** 43, 44
blackbird, red-winged, 16, **16,** 17
bread, 22, 23
buckwheat, 41

cardinal, northern, 11, **11,** 31
chickadee, 5, 8–10, 15, 41
    black-capped, **5,** 6, **8,** 9, 10
    Carolina, 9, **9**
    chestnut-backed, 10, **10**
    mountain, 10, **10**
corn, 31, 41
cover, 44
cowbird, brown-headed, 16, 18, **18**
crow, American, 34, **34**
crow family, 32–35

digestion, 6, 24
dove
    mourning, 24, **24, 42**
    rock (pigeon), 25, **25**
down (as insulation), 5

fat for birds, *see* suet
feathers (as insulation), 5
feeders, 42–44, **42, 43, 44**
finch, 36–40
    gold-, 36, **36,** 38, 39
    house, 36, 37, **37,** 38, **43**
    purple, 38, **38**
flicker, northern, 14, **14**
flocks, 4, 9, 10, 15, 16, 17, 22, 25, 26, 28, 31, 34, 36, 38
food for birds, 41–42
fruit, 20, 21, 22, 23, 25, 40

goldfinch, *see* finch, gold-
grackle, common, 16, 17, **17**
grosbeak, evening, **3,** 40, **40, 48**

irruptions, 4, 38

jay
    blue, 32, **32,** 33
    scrub, 33, **33**
    Stellar's, 33, **33**
junco, dark-eyed, **4,** 30, **30, 46**

magpie, black-billed, 35, **35**
migration, 4, 21, 23, 29, 30
    changes in, 6, 16, 22
millet, 41
milo, 41
mockingbird, northern, 20, **20,** 21

niger seed, 36, 41, 43
nuthatch, 15
    red-breasted, 15, **15**
    white-breasted, 15, **15**

peanut butter, 19, 20, 42, 44
pigeon, *see* dove, rock

ranges, changes in, 9, 11, 13, 17, 19, 24, 32, 37
redpoll, 6
    common, 39, **39**
robin, American, 22, **22**
roosting, 5, 16, 34

siskin, pine, 38, 39, **39**
snowbird, *see* junco, dark-eyed
sorghum, *see* milo
sparrow, 25, 26, 28–30, 31
    chipping, 28, 29, **29**
    English, *see* sparrow, house
    fox, 28, **28**
    Harris's, 29, **29**
    house, 25, 26, **26**
    song, 28, **28**
    tree, American, 28, **28**
    white-crowned, 30, **30, 45**
    white-throated, 30, **30, 45**

starling, European, 25, 27, **27**
suet, 12, 13, 19, 20, 21, 22, 23, 31,
    41–42, 44
sunflower seeds, 9, 11, 15, 33, 36, 40,
    41, 43
survival in winter, 4–6

temperatures (of birds), 5, 6
thistle seed, *see* niger seed
thrasher, brown, 21, **21**
thrush, 22
    varied, 23, **23**
titmouse, 8–10, 15, 41

plain, 10, **10**
    tufted, **8,** 9, 10, **44**
towhee, rufous-sided, 31, **31**

wanderers, 4, 38–40
water for birds, 42
wheat, 41
woodpecker, 5, 12–14, 41
    downy, 12, **12**
    hairy, **2,** 12, **12**
    red-bellied, 13, **13**
wren, Carolina, 19, **19**